Auditory Processing
of
"WH" Words

Jean Gilliam DeGaetano

Great Ideas for Teaching, Inc. P.O. Box 444 Wrightsville Beach, NC   28480

ISBN 1-886143-28-5

AUDITORY PROCESSING OF "WH" WORDS

Jean Gilliam DeGaetano
Illustrations: Clip Art: Graphic Products Corporation

Components:

62 reproducible masters
31 student worksheets
31 corresponding instructor's worksheets

Directions for use are provided on each copy of the instructor's worksheet.

Illustrations:

"Clip Art" was used to demonstrate how beneficial clip art can be to professionals who are teaching specific skills that require visual reinforcement.

Self Evaluation:

Students should evaluate their own listening skills, following the instructor's directions.

Purpose:

The purpose of the unit is to provide practice in comprehending questions that begin with "wh" words.

Directions:

Before beginning, each student should be given a copy of the student worksheet that corresponds to the instructor's worksheet. Start with any picture and its group of questions. Ask the entire group of questions under a picture before going on to another picture. The students are to look at their working copy while they listen to the questions and answer them aloud. Assistance should be given to the students if their answers are incorrect. After each page is completed, the students should evaluate their own listening skills and circle the number of smiles they feel they have earned for good listening. One smile is for good listening. Two smiles are for very good listening. Three smiles are for great listening.

STUDENT WORKSHEET

Name: _____

AUDITORY PROCESSING OF "WH" WORDS

INSTRUCTOR'S WORKSHEET

<u>DIRECTIONS:</u> Before beginning, each student should be given a copy of the student worksheet that corresponds to this instructor's worksheet. Start with any picture and its group of questions. Ask the entire group of questions under a picture before going on to another picture. The students are to look at their working copy while they listen to the questions and answer them aloud. Assistance should be given to the students if their answers are incorrect. After each page is completed, the students should evaluate their own listening skills and circle the number of smiles they feel they have earned for good listening. One smile is for <u>good listening</u>. Two smiles are for <u>very good listening</u>. Three smiles are for <u>great listening</u>.

Who is vacuuming?
What is she using to vacuum?
Why do people use a vacuum?
Where does the dirt go?
What makes the motor run?

Who is sweeping?
What is she using?
Why do people sweep floors?
What part of a broom do you hold?
Where is the broom kept?

Who is digging?
What is she using to dig?
Where is she digging a hole?
Why is she digging a hole?
What will she put in the hole?

Who is mowing?
What is he using to mow?
What is he mowing?
Why do people cut grass?
Where do the grass clippings fall?

Great Ideas for Teaching!   AUDITORY PROCESSING OF "WH" WORDS

2

Name: _____

INSTRUCTOR'S WORKSHEET

<u>DIRECTIONS:</u> Before beginning, each student should be given a copy of the student worksheet that corresponds to this instructor's worksheet. Start with any picture and its group of questions. Ask the entire group of questions under a picture before going on to another picture. The students are to look at their working copy while they listen to the questions and answer them aloud. Assistance should be given to the students if their answers are incorrect. After each page is completed, the students should evaluate their own listening skills and circle the number of smiles they feel they have earned for good listening. One smile is for <u>good listening</u>. Two smiles are for <u>very good listening</u>. Three smiles are for <u>great listening</u>.

Who is jumping?
What is he jumping on?
Why is he jumping on the pogo stick?
Where do you use a pogo stick?
What part of the stick is he holding?

Who has her hair in a braid?
What is she riding on?
Why is she holding the handlebar?
Where do you use a scooter?
Why is one foot off the scooter?

Who is skating?
What kind of skates is she wearing?
Why is she wearing a helmet?
Where is a good place to skate?

Who has on a striped shirt?
What is he riding?
Why does he only have one foot on the skateboard?
Where do you use a skateboard?

Great Ideas for Teaching!   AUDITORY PROCESSING OF "WH" WORDS

STUDENT WORKSHEET

Name: _____

☺   ☺   ☺

ICE COLD
LEMONADE
25¢

INSTRUCTOR'S WORKSHEET

DIRECTIONS: Before beginning, each student should be given a copy of the student worksheet that corresponds to this instructor's worksheet. Start with any picture and its group of questions. Ask the entire group of questions under a picture before going on to another picture. The students are to look at their working copy while they listen to the questions and answer them aloud. Assistance should be given to the students if their answers are incorrect. After each page is completed, the students should evaluate their own listening skills and circle the number of smiles they feel they have earned for good listening. One smile is for good listening. Two smiles are for very good listening. Three smiles are for great listening.

Who is holding a tray?
What is on the tray?
Why does she need a tray?
What would happen if she dropped the tray?
Where do you think she is going?

Who is standing near a door?
What is he doing?
Why is he ringing the doorbell?
What is he holding in his hand?
What do you think is in the box?

Who is sitting on a chair?
What do you think she is doing?
Where will she pour the lemonade?
Why do you think she is sad?
Why is she selling lemonade?

Who is taking something out of the oven?
What is he taking out of the oven?
Why did he not use his hands?
Where do you think he is?
When do you eat pizza?

Great Ideas for Teaching!   AUDITORY PROCESSING OF "WH" WORDS

STUDENT WORKSHEET

Name: _____

Great Ideas for Teaching!   AUDITORY PROCESSING OF "WH" WORDS

7

INSTRUCTOR'S WORKSHEET

DIRECTIONS: Before beginning, each student should be given a copy of the student worksheet that corresponds to this instructor's worksheet. Start with any picture and its group of questions. Ask the entire group of questions under a picture before going on to another picture. The students are to look at their working copy while they listen to the questions and answer them aloud. Assistance should be given to the students if their answers are incorrect. After each page is completed, the students should evaluate their own listening skills and circle the number of smiles they feel they have earned for good listening. One smile is for good listening. Two smiles are for very good listening. Three smiles are for great listening.

Who is holding a spatula and plate?
What is he wearing on his head?
What is he doing?
Where are the pancakes?
Why is he holding a plate?

Who is standing on a chair?
Why is she standing on a chair?
What is she doing?
Where is the cake mix?
Why is she using the beater?

Who is cooking something outside?
What is he cooking?
Where is he cooking the hot dog?
When will the hot dog be done?
Why do you not touch fire?

Who is eating something?
What is he eating?
Where is the hot dog?
What do you put on a hot dog?
When will the hot dog be all gone?

Great Ideas for Teaching!   AUDITORY PROCESSING OF "WH" WORDS

8

Name: _____

INSTRUCTOR'S WORKSHEET

DIRECTIONS: Before beginning, each student should be given a copy of the student worksheet that corresponds to this instructor's worksheet. Start with any picture and its group of questions. Ask the entire group of questions under a picture before going on to another picture. The students are to look at their working copy while they listen to the questions and answer them aloud. Assistance should be given to the students if their answers are incorrect. After each page is completed, the students should evaluate their own listening skills and circle the number of smiles they feel they have earned for good listening. One smile is for good listening. Two smiles are for very good listening. Three smiles are for great listening.

Who is eating something from a big bowl?
What are the girls eating?
What is popcorn made from?
Where do you pop popcorn?
Why are they eating popcorn?

Who is holding a spoon?
Why is he holding a spoon?
What is he eating?
Where is he sitting?
Why is he in a high chair?

Which children are eating something cold?
Who is eating with one hand?
Where is his other hand?
Who is licking something?
What is she licking?

Which children are eating lunch?
What are the children eating?
Who has two cookies on a plate?
Where are the children sitting?
What is in the middle of the table?

Great Ideas for Teaching!   AUDITORY PROCESSING OF "WH" WORDS

10

STUDENT WORKSHEET

Name: _____

INSTRUCTOR'S WORKSHEET

<u>DIRECTIONS:</u> Before beginning, each student should be given a copy of the student worksheet that corresponds to this instructor's worksheet. Start with any picture and its group of questions. Ask the entire group of questions under a picture before going on to another picture. The students are to look at their working copy while they listen to the questions and answer them aloud. Assistance should be given to the students if their answers are incorrect. After each page is completed, the students should evaluate their own listening skills and circle the number of smiles they feel they have earned for good listening? One smile is for <u>good listening</u>. Two smiles are for <u>very good listening</u>. Three smiles are for <u>great listening</u>.

Who is holding a scrub brush?
Who is holding a hose?
What is being washed?
Where are they?
Why do you wash a dog?

Who is in the doghouse?
What is beside the boy?
What are they doing?
Why does a doghouse have a roof?
Where are doghouses kept?

Who is painting at the easel?
Who is sitting?
What do you think they will draw?
Where are they?
Why does the girl need a brush?

Who is getting wet from a sprinkler?
What is spraying the water?
Where do you think he is?
What is the boy wearing?
Why is he wearing a bathing suit?

Great Ideas for Teaching!   AUDITORY PROCESSING OF "WH" WORDS

STUDENT WORKSHEET

Name: _____

INSTRUCTOR'S WORKSHEET

DIRECTIONS: Before beginning, each student should be given a copy of the student worksheet that corresponds to this instructor's worksheet. Start with any picture and its group of questions. Ask the entire group of questions under a picture before going on to another picture. The students are to look at their working copy while they listen to the questions and answer them aloud. Assistance should be given to the students if their answers are incorrect. After each page is completed, the students should evaluate their own listening skills and circle the number of smiles they feel they have earned for good listening. One smile is for good listening. Two smiles are for very good listening. Three smiles are for great listening.

Who is talking to something?
What is she playing with?
Where is the bear?
What part of a wagon rolls?
Why does a wagon have a handle?

Who is on a skateboard?
What makes a skateboard roll?
Where do people ride skateboards?
Why do people ride on them?
Why must a person be careful on a skateboard?

Who is painting something?
What is she painting?
What is she painting with?
Where is she painting her water colors?
Why is she using a paintbrush?

Who is riding in something?
Where is the child sitting?
What is the child holding?
Why is he holding the handle?
What turns when the wagon moves?

Great Ideas for Teaching!   AUDITORY PROCESSING OF "WH" WORDS

STUDENT WORKSHEET

Name: _____

INSTRUCTOR'S WORKSHEET

DIRECTIONS: Before beginning, each student should be given a copy of the student worksheet that corresponds to this instructor's worksheet. Start with any picture and its group of questions. Ask the entire group of questions under a picture before going on to another picture. The students are to look at their working copy while they listen to the questions and answer them aloud. Assistance should be given to the students if their answers are incorrect. After each page is completed, the students should evaluate their own listening skills and circle the number of smiles they feel they have earned for good listening. One smile is for good listening. Two smiles are for very good listening. Three smiles are for great listening.

Who is splashing?
What is the baby splashing?
What is the water in?
Why is the baby in the tub?
Why is the baby laughing?

Who is touching something?
What is being touched?
Where did the baby touch the cat?
Why is the baby touching the cat?
What sound does a cat make?

Who is throwing something?
Who will catch something?
What will she catch?
Where will the ball land if she doesn't catch it?

Who is blowing up something?
What is he blowing up?
Why do you blow into a balloon?
Where will the balloon go if he lets go of it?

Great Ideas for Teaching!

AUDITORY PROCESSING OF "WH" WORDS

STUDENT WORKSHEET

Name: _____

Great Ideas for Teaching!   AUDITORY PROCESSING OF "WH" WORDS

17

INSTRUCTOR'S WORKSHEET

DIRECTIONS: Before beginning, each student should be given a copy of the student worksheet that corresponds to this instructor's worksheet. Start with any picture and its group of questions. Ask the entire group of questions under a picture before going on to another picture. The students are to look at their working copy while they listen to the questions and answer them aloud. Assistance should be given to the students if their answers are incorrect. After each page is completed, the students should evaluate their own listening skills and circle the number of smiles they feel they have earned for good listening. One smile is for good listening. Two smiles are for very good listening. Three smiles are for great listening.

Who has on black shorts?
Why is her hair in a ponytail?
What is she doing?
What does she have on her feet?
Where do you think she is?

Who has on a flowered skirt?
What is she doing?
What is tied in her hair?
What is on her feet?
Why is she wearing shoes?

Who has freckles?
What is she doing?
Why is she wearing shoes and socks?
When did she run? In summer or winter?
Where is she running?

Which child has short hair?
Why is he smiling?
What is he doing?
What is he wearing?
Where is he going?

Great Ideas for Teaching!   AUDITORY PROCESSING OF "WH" WORDS

STUDENT WORKSHEET

Name: _____

 ☺ ☺ ☺

Great Ideas for Teaching!   AUDITORY PROCESSING OF "WH" WORDS

19

INSTRUCTOR'S WORKSHEET

<u>DIRECTIONS:</u> Before beginning, each student should be given a copy of the student worksheet that corresponds to this instructor's worksheet. Start with any picture and its group of questions. Ask the entire group of questions under a picture before going on to another picture. The students are to look at their working copy while they listen to the questions and answer them aloud. Assistance should be given to the students if their answers are incorrect. After each page is completed, the students should evaluate their own listening skills and circle the number of smiles they feel they have earned for good listening. One smile is for <u>good listening</u>. Two smiles are for <u>very good listening</u>. Three smiles are for <u>great listening</u>.

Who is holding her nose?
Why is she holding her nose?
What do you think she is doing?
Where do you think she is?
What is she wearing?

Who is floating in something?
What is she floating in?
Where is she floating?
Why do you think she is in the float?
What animal does the float look like?

Who is wearing a black bathing suit?
Where is she standing?
What is she going to do?
Why do you think she has her hands together?

Who is diving?
Where is he diving from?
What is he diving into?
When you dive, what part of your body goes in the water first?

STUDENT WORKSHEET

Name: _____

   ☺   ☺

Great Ideas for Teaching!   AUDITORY PROCESSING OF "WH" WORDS

21

INSTRUCTOR'S WORKSHEET

<u>DIRECTIONS:</u> Before beginning, each student should be given a copy of the student worksheet that corresponds to this instructor's worksheet. Start with any picture and its group of questions. Ask the entire group of questions under a picture before going on to another picture. The students are to look at their working copy while they listen to the questions and answer them aloud. Assistance should be given to the students if their answers are incorrect. After each page is completed, the students should evaluate their own listening skills and circle the number of smiles they feel they have earned for good listening. One smile is for <u>good listening</u>. Two smiles are for <u>very good listening</u>. Three smiles are for <u>great listening</u>.

Who is standing near a base?
What is she doing?
What does she have on her hand?
Why is she wearing a ball glove?
Where do you play ball?

Who is wearing a striped ball cap?
What is she doing?
Where do you think she threw the ball?
Why did she throw the ball?
What kind of ball did she throw?

Who is wearing a protective vest?
Why does his hat look funny?
What does he have on his face?
Why does he wear a mask?
Where does an umpire stand?

Who is holding a bat?
Where is she holding the bat?
What will she do with the bat?
What will she do after she hits the
ball with the bat?

Great Ideas for Teaching!   AUDITORY PROCESSING OF "WH" WORDS

22

STUDENT WORKSHEET

Name: _____

DIRECTIONS: Before beginning, each student should be given a copy of the student worksheet that corresponds to this instructor's worksheet. Start with any picture and its group of questions. Ask the entire group of questions under a picture before going on to another picture. The students are to look at their working copy while they listen to the questions and answer them aloud. Assistance should be given to the students if their answers are incorrect. After each page is completed, the students should evaluate their own listening skills and circle the number of smiles they feel they have earned for good listening. One smile is for good listening. Two smiles are for very good listening. Three smiles are for great listening.

Who is feeding the calf?
What is the calf eating?
What is the little girl wearing on her feet?
Where does a baby calf live?
Why do you think she is feeding the baby calf?

Who is riding something with pedals?
What is she riding?
Where do you think she is going?
Why does she have two hands on the handlebars?

Who is riding something with one wheel?
What is she riding?
What sound does a real horse make?
Where does a real horse live?
What does the girl have on her head?

Who is kneeling on the floor?
What is he doing?
Where is he drawing a picture?
What is he using to draw?
What is he drawing a picture of?

Great Ideas for Teaching!   AUDITORY PROCESSING OF "WH" WORDS

24

STUDENT WORKSHEET

Name: _____

☺   ☺   ☺

INSTRUCTOR'S WORKSHEET

DIRECTIONS: Before beginning, each student should be given a copy of the student worksheet that corresponds to this instructor's worksheet. Start with any picture and its group of questions. Ask the entire group of questions under a picture before going on to another picture. The students are to look at their working copy while they listen to the questions and answer them aloud. Assistance should be given to the students if their answers are incorrect. After each page is completed, the students should evaluate their own listening skills and circle the number of smiles they feel they have earned for good listening. One smile is for good listening. Two smiles are for very good listening. Three smiles are for great listening.

Who has on striped shorts?
What is the boy doing?
Where is his head?
Where do you think he is doing this?
Why are his feet in the air?

Who is wearing a hat?
What is she holding in her hand?
Why does a balloon float in the air?
Where will the balloon go if she lets
lets go of it?

Who is waving?
Who do you think he is waving at?
What does he have in his hand?
Where is the pail?
Where can you use a pail and shovel?

Who is pulling a toy?
What part of the toy is the girl holding?
What animal does the toy look like?
Why does the toy have wheels?
Where are the wheels?

Great Ideas for Teaching!   AUDITORY PROCESSING OF "WH" WORDS

STUDENT WORKSHEET

Name: _____

INSTRUCTOR'S WORKSHEET

DIRECTIONS: Before beginning, each student should be given a copy of the student worksheet that corresponds to this instructor's worksheet. Start with any picture and its group of questions. Ask the entire group of questions under a picture before going on to another picture. The students are to look at their working copy while they listen to the questions and answer them aloud. Assistance should be given to the students if their answers are incorrect. After each page is completed, the students should evaluate their own listening skills and circle the number of smiles they feel they have earned for good listening. One smile is for good listening. Two smiles are for very good listening. Three smiles are for great listening.

Which children are building something?
What are they building?
Who is making a head for the snowman?
What will happen to the snowman when the sun comes out?

Who is working outside?
What is he doing?
Why is he shoveling snow?
Where is he shoveling snow?
Why does he have on a scarf and hat?

Which children are throwing something?
What are the children throwing?
Where are the children keeping their snowballs?
Why do the children have on coats and hats?
What are the children standing behind?

Great Ideas for Teaching!   AUDITORY PROCESSING OF "WH" WORDS

28

STUDENT WORKSHEET

Name: _____

INSTRUCTOR'S WORKSHEET

DIRECTIONS: Before beginning, each student should be given a copy of the student worksheet that corresponds to this instructor's worksheet. Start with any picture and its group of questions. Ask the entire group of questions under a picture before going on to another picture. The students are to look at their working copy while they listen to the questions and answer them aloud. Assistance should be given to the students if their answers are incorrect. After each page is completed, the students should evaluate their own listening skills and circle the number of smiles they feel they have earned for good listening. One smile is for good listening. Two smiles are for very good listening. Three smiles are for great listening.

Who is playing hockey?
What is he wearing on his feet?
Where do you play hockey - on ice or dirt?
Why is he holding a hockey stick?
What will he hit with the hockey stick?

Who is bouncing something?
What is he bouncing?
What will he do with the ball besides bouncing it ?
Where do you throw a basketball?

Who is playing golf?
What is the girl holding?
What do you do with a golf club?
What kind of ball is she using?
Where do people play golf?

Who is holding something with strings?
What is he holding?
Why does he have a tennis racket?
Where do people play tennis?
What kind of ball will he use?

Great Ideas for Teaching!   AUDITORY PROCESSING OF "WH" WORDS

30

Name: _____

Great Ideas for Teaching!   AUDITORY PROCESSING OF "WH" WORDS

31

INSTRUCTOR'S WORKSHEET

DIRECTIONS: Before beginning, each student should be given a copy of the student worksheet that corresponds to this instructor's worksheet. Start with any picture and its group of questions. Ask the entire group of questions under a picture before going on to another picture. The students are to look at their working copy while they listen to the questions and answer them aloud. Assistance should be given to the students if their answers are incorrect. After each page is completed, the students should evaluate their own listening skills and circle the number of smiles they feel they have earned for good listening. One smile is for good listening. Two smiles are for very good listening. Three smiles are for great listening.

Where do you see two children?
What are they doing?
Who is running in front?
Why do you think they are running?
What do they have on their feet?

Who is riding a skateboard?
What part of a skateboard rolls?
Why do skateboards have wheels?
Where do people ride skateboards -
inside or outside?

Who is sweeping?
What is he sweeping with?
What part of the broom is he holding?
What part of the broom touches the floor?
Why do you think he is sweeping?

Who is painting?
What is he painting?
What is he painting on?
What is he painting with?
Where are the paints?

Great Ideas for Teaching!　　　　　　　　　　AUDITORY PROCESSING OF "WH" WORDS

STUDENT WORKSHEET

Name: _____

INSTRUCTOR'S WORKSHEET

DIRECTIONS: Before beginning, each student should be given a copy of the student worksheet that corresponds to this instructor's worksheet. Start with any picture and its group of questions. Ask the entire group of questions under a picture before going on to another picture. The students are to look at their working copy while they listen to the questions and answer them aloud. Assistance should be given to the students if their answers are incorrect. After each page is completed, the students should evaluate their own listening skills and circle the number of smiles they feel they have earned for good listening. One smile is for good listening. Two smiles are for very good listening. Three smiles are for great listening.

Who is holding something made of wood?
What is he holding?
What will he do with the hammer?
Why is he playing with the hammer?
Where is the baby sitting?

Who has a bow in her hair?
What is she doing?
Where is the baby coloring?
Why will the baby's mother be unhappy?
Where should you use a crayon?

Who is chasing something?
What is he chasing?
Why is he chasing the duck?
Why is the duck flapping its wings?
Where do you think the duck is going?

Who is wearing a hat?
What is he petting?
Why is he petting the puppy?
Where is the puppy sitting?
Why is the boy happy?

Great Ideas for Teaching!   AUDITORY PROCESSING OF "WH" WORDS

34

STUDENT WORKSHEET

Name: _____

☺   ☺   ☺

INSTRUCTOR'S WORKSHEET

DIRECTIONS: Before beginning, each student should be given a copy of the student worksheet that corresponds to this instructor's worksheet. Start with any picture and its group of questions. Ask the entire group of questions under a picture before going on to another picture. The students are to look at their working copy while they listen to the questions and answer them aloud. Assistance should be given to the students if their answers are incorrect. After each page is completed, the students should evaluate their own listening skills and circle the number of smiles they feel they have earned for good listening. One smile is for good listening. Two smiles are for very good listening. Three smiles are for great listening.

Who is sitting on a chair?
What is she doing?
Where is she writing?
What is she wearing on her face?
Why do people wear glasses?

Who is sitting on the ground?
What is he leaning against?
What does he have in his mouth?
Where is his book?
Why is he not reading the book?

Who is kneeling on the ground?
Why is he kneeling?
What is he doing?
Where do the marbles roll?
Why do marbles roll?

Which children are running?
Who is running in front?
Why do you think they are running?
What do they have on their feet?
Where are they running?

Great Ideas for Teaching!   AUDITORY PROCESSING OF "WH" WORDS

STUDENT WORKSHEET

Name: _____

INSTRUCTOR'S WORKSHEET

DIRECTIONS: Before beginning, each student should be given a copy of the student worksheet that corresponds to this instructor's worksheet. Start with any picture and its group of questions. Ask the entire group of questions under a picture before going on to another picture. The students are to look at their working copy while they listen to the questions and answer them aloud. Assistance should be given to the students if their answers are incorrect. After each page is completed, the students should evaluate their own listening skills and circle the number of smiles they feel they have earned for good listening. One smile is for good listening. Two smiles are for very good listening. Three smiles are for great listening.

Who is playing with a ball?
What is she doing with the ball?
Where do you play with a ball?
Why does a ball roll?
Why is the girl happy?

Who is waving?
What is he holding in his hand?
What will he do with the shovel?
Where will he put the dirt?
Where does the dirt come from?

Where do you see three children playing?
What are they playing in?
Who is putting sand in a bucket?
Why can't the boy in the hat help shovel?
What is the baby holding in his hand?

Great Ideas for Teaching! AUDITORY PROCESSING OF "WH" WORDS

STUDENT WORKSHEET

Name: _____

☺   ☺   ☺

Great Ideas for Teaching!   AUDITORY PROCESSING OF "WH" WORDS

39

INSTRUCTOR'S WORKSHEET

DIRECTIONS: Before beginning, each student should be given a copy of the student worksheet that corresponds to this instructor's worksheet. Start with any picture and its group of questions. Ask the entire group of questions under a picture before going on to another picture. The students are to look at their working copy while they listen to the questions and answer them aloud. Assistance should be given to the students if their answers are incorrect. After each page is completed, the students should evaluate their own listening skills and circle the number of smiles they feel they have earned for good listening. One smile is for <u>good listening</u>. Two smiles are for <u>very good listening</u>. Three smiles are for <u>great listening</u>.

Who is holding a bat?
Why is he holding a bat?
What kind of ball will he hit?
Where is homeplate?

Who is wearing flowered shorts?
What does he have on his hand?
Why did he miss the ball?
Where will the ball land?

Who is running after something?
What is the boy looking for?
What does the boy have on his hand?
Where do you think the ball is?

Who is tossing a ball?
Why is the boy sad?
What is he wearing on his head?
Where is his hand that you can't see?

Great Ideas for Teaching!   AUDITORY PROCESSING OF "WH" WORDS

Name: _____

INSTRUCTOR'S WORKSHEET

DIRECTIONS: Before beginning, each student should be given a copy of the student worksheet that corresponds to this instructor's worksheet. Start with any picture and its group of questions. Ask the entire group of questions under a picture before going on to another picture. The students are to look at their working copy while they listen to the questions and answer them aloud. Assistance should be given to the students if their answers are incorrect. After each page is completed, the students should evaluate their own listening skills and circle the number of smiles they feel they have earned for good listening. One smile is for <u>good listening</u>. Two smiles are for <u>very good listening</u>. Three smiles are for <u>great listening</u>.

Which children are playing football?
What are they wearing on their heads?
Why is one boy standing behind the other boy?
Where do you play football - inside or outside?

Who is bouncing a ball?
What kind of ball is she bouncing?
Where do you play basketball?
What does she have on her feet?

Which children are running after a ball?
What kind of ball are they playing with?
Who is going to kick the ball first?
Where do you play soccer - on a field or court?

Who is hitting something?
What is she using to hit the ball?
Where do you play golf?
Why is she wearing a sun visor?

Great Ideas for Teaching!   AUDITORY PROCESSING OF "WH" WORDS

42

STUDENT WORKSHEET

Name: _____

INSTRUCTOR'S WORKSHEET

DIRECTIONS: Before beginning, each student should be given a copy of the student worksheet that corresponds to this instructor's worksheet. Start with any picture and its group of questions. Ask the entire group of questions under a picture before going on to another picture. The students are to look at their working copy while they listen to the questions and answer them aloud. Assistance should be given to the students if their answers are incorrect. After each page is completed, the students should evaluate their own listening skills and circle the number of smiles they feel they have earned for good listening. One smile is for good listening. Two smiles are for very good listening. Three smiles are for great listening.

Who is washing something?
What is he washing?
What is he using to wash the wall?
Why is he washing the wall?
Where is the soap and water?

Who is watering something?
What is she using to water the flower?
Why is she watering the flower?
When will she be finished watering?
Where do flowers grow?

Who is playing with a toy?
What kind of toy is he playing with?
Why is he crawling on the floor?
Where is he holding the truck?
What part of the truck rolls?

Who is standing on something?
What is he standing on?
Why is he standing on the ladder?
What is the boy picking off the tree?
Where is he putting the apples?

Great Ideas for Teaching!

AUDITORY PROCESSING OF "WH" WORDS

Name: _____

☺   ☺   ☺

INSTRUCTOR'S WORKSHEET

DIRECTIONS: Before beginning, each student should be given a copy of the student worksheet that corresponds to this instructor's worksheet. Start with any picture and its group of questions. Ask the entire group of questions under a picture before going on to another picture. The students are to look at their working copy while they listen to the questions and answer them aloud. Assistance should be given to the students if their answers are incorrect. After each page is completed, the students should evaluate their own listening skills and circle the number of smiles they feel they have earned for good listening. One smile is for <u>good listening</u>. Two smiles are for <u>very good listening</u>. Three smiles are for <u>great listening</u>.

Who has a bow in her hair?
What kind of instrument is she playing?
What is she using to play the violin?
What part of the violin makes music?
Where is she holding the violin?

Who is wearing a striped shirt?
What is he doing?
What kind of instrument is he playing?
Where does the music come out?
Which part of the trombone moves?

Which children are wearing uniforms?
Why are they wearing uniforms?
Where is the person holding a baton - first or last?
What kind of instrument is the tall boy playing?
Who is wearing a pair of glasses?

Great Ideas for Teaching!   AUDITORY PROCESSING OF "WH" WORDS

46

Name: _____

☺   ☺   ☺

Great Ideas for Teaching!   AUDITORY PROCESSING OF "WH" WORDS

47

INSTRUCTOR'S WORKSHEET

DIRECTIONS: Before beginning, each student should be given a copy of the student worksheet that corresponds to this instructor's worksheet. Start with any picture and its group of questions. Ask the entire group of questions under a picture before going on to another picture. The students are to look at their working copy while they listen to the questions and answer them aloud. Assistance should be given to the students if their answers are incorrect. After each page is completed, the students should evaluate their own listening skills and circle the number of smiles they feel they have earned for good listening. One smile is for good listening. Two smiles are for very good listening. Three smiles are for great listening.

Who is pushing something?
What is the girl pushing?
Where do you use a lawnmower?
Why do you use a lawnmower?
Where does the grass go after it is cut?

Who is playing an instrument?
What is he playing?
What does he use to play the piano?
Where are his feet?
Why is he sitting on the stool?

Who is wearing sunglasses?
What is she carrying?
What is inside the basket?
Where did the leaves come from?
Why is she using two hands to carry the basket?

Who is using a garden tool?
What is he using?
Why is he using a rake?
Where are the leaves?
When do you rake leaves?

Great Ideas for Teaching!   AUDITORY PROCESSING OF "WH" WORDS

48

STUDENT WORKSHEET

Name: _____

INSTRUCTOR'S WORKSHEET

DIRECTIONS: Before beginning, each student should be given a copy of the student worksheet that corresponds to this instructor's worksheet. Start with any picture and its group of questions. Ask the entire group of questions under a picture before going on to another picture. The students are to look at their working copy while they listen to the questions and answer them aloud. Assistance should be given to the students if their answers are incorrect. After each page is completed, the students should evaluate their own listening skills and circle the number of smiles they feel they have earned for good listening. One smile is for good listening. Two smiles are for very good listening. Three smiles are for great listening.

Who is washing something?
What is she washing?
Why is she washing the window?
Where is she washing the window - on the inside or outside?

Who is standing inside at a window?
What is she doing?
What is she using to water the flowers?
Why is she watering the flowers?
Where are the flowers?

Who is resting?
Why do you think she is resting?
What was she doing before she rested?
What kind of chair is she sitting in?
Where is the vacuum?

Who is pushing something?
What is she pushing?
Why do you use a vacuum cleaner?
Where do you use a vacuum cleaner?
Where does the dirt go?

STUDENT WORKSHEET

Name: _____

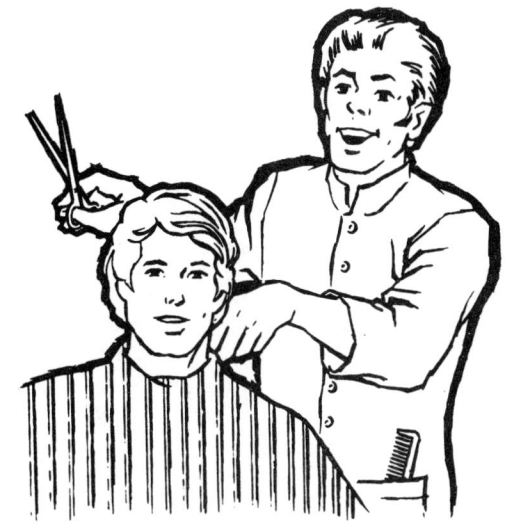

INSTRUCTOR'S WORKSHEET

DIRECTIONS: Before beginning, each student should be given a copy of the student worksheet that corresponds to this instructor's worksheet. Start with any picture and its group of questions. Ask the entire group of questions under a picture before going on to another picture. The students are to look at their working copy while they listen to the questions and answer them aloud. Assistance should be given to the students if their answers are incorrect. After each page is completed, the students should evaluate their own listening skills and circle the number of smiles they feel they have earned for good listening. One smile is for good listening. Two smiles are for very good listening. Three smiles are for great listening.

Who is taking a picture?
What is he using to take a picture?
Why is he holding the camera with two hands?
What would happen if he dropped the camera?
Why do you take pictures?

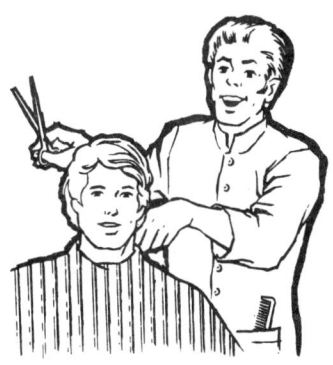

Who is cutting someone's hair?
What does he use to cut hair?
Why do you get a haircut?
Where is the comb?
What will he do with the comb?

Who is wearing a hat?
Where do you think this man works?
What is he pointing at?
Where do you buy meat ?
Where do you cook meat?

Who is pumping gas?
Where do you think the man is?
Where is he putting the gas?
Why do you put gas in a car?
What happens if a car runs out of gas?

Great Ideas for Teaching!   AUDITORY PROCESSING OF "WH" WORDS

Name: _____

 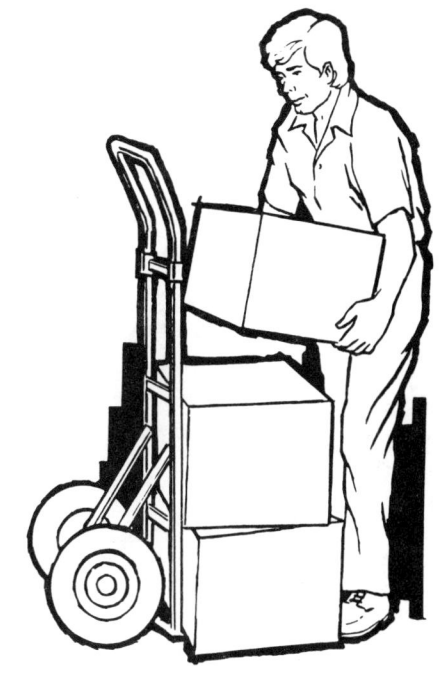

Great Ideas for Teaching!   AUDITORY PROCESSING OF "WH" WORDS

53

INSTRUCTOR'S WORKSHEET

DIRECTIONS: Before beginning, each student should be given a copy of the student worksheet that corresponds to this instructor's worksheet. Start with any picture and its group of questions. Ask the entire group of questions under a picture before going on to another picture. The students are to look at their working copy while they listen to the questions and answer them aloud. Assistance should be given to the students if their answers are incorrect. After each page is completed, the students should evaluate their own listening skills and circle the number of smiles they feel they have earned for good listening. One smile is for <u>good listening</u>. Two smiles are for <u>very good listening</u>. Three smiles are for <u>great listening</u>.

Who is wearing a hat?
What is he carrying?
Why is he using both hands?
Where did he get the boxes?

Who is lifting a box?
Where is he putting the box?
What will he use to move the boxes?
What makes the cart roll?

Who is pouring something out of a bag?
What is he pouring out of the bag?
Where is he putting the charcoal?
What do you do with charcoal?

Who is riding on something?
What is he riding on?
Where do you use a riding lawnmower?
Why do you need a riding lawnmower?

Great Ideas for Teaching!   AUDITORY PROCESSING OF "WH" WORDS

Name: _____

DIRECTIONS: Before beginning, each student should be given a copy of the student worksheet that corresponds to this instructor's worksheet. Start with any picture and its group of questions. Ask the entire group of questions under a picture before going on to another picture. The students are to look at their working copy while they listen to the questions and answer them aloud. Assistance should be given to the students if their answers are incorrect. After each page is completed, the students should evaluate their own listening skills and circle the number of smiles they feel they have earned for good listening. One smile is for good listening. Two smiles are for very good listening. Three smiles are for great listening.

Who is setting the table?
What is she putting beside the plate?
Where would you find a table and dishes?
When do you use plates and glasses?

Who is wearing an apron?
What is she doing?
Where is she putting the folded clothes?
Where did she wash the clothes?

Who is pushing a shopping cart?
What kind of stores have shopping carts?
What do you put in a shopping cart?
Why do you need a shopping cart?

Who is taking something out of a bag?
What is in the bags?
Where did she buy the groceries?
Where will she put the groceries?

Great Ideas for Teaching!   AUDITORY PROCESSING OF "WH" WORDS

56

Name: _____

INSTRUCTOR'S WORKSHEET

DIRECTIONS: Before beginning, each student should be given a copy of the student worksheet that corresponds to this instructor's worksheet. Start with any picture and its group of questions. Ask the entire group of questions under a picture before going on to another picture. The students are to look at their working copy while they listen to the questions and answer them aloud. Assistance should be given to the students if their answers are incorrect. After each page is completed, the students should evaluate their own listening skills and circle the number of smiles they feel they have earned for good listening. One smile is for good listening. Two smiles are for very good listening. Three smiles are for great listening.

Which children are building something?
What are they building?
Where are they building the sandcastle?
When do you go to the beach - in summer or winter?

Who is wearing an apron?
What is he doing?
Where is he cooking the food?
What is he cooking on the grill?
Why is he using a spatula?

Which children are playing in the water?
What are they playing with?
Where do you think they are playing?
Why do they have on bathing suits?
Who is closest to the beach ball?

Who is fishing?
What is he using to fish with?
Where is he standing?
Why is he wearing tall boots?
What did he drive?

Great Ideas for Teaching!   AUDITORY PROCESSING OF "WH" WORDS

58

STUDENT WORKSHEET

Name: _____

INSTRUCTOR'S WORKSHEET

DIRECTIONS: Before beginning, each student should be given a copy of the student worksheet that corresponds to this instructor's worksheet. Start with any picture and its group of questions. Ask the entire group of questions under a picture before going on to another picture. The students are to look at their working copy while they listen to the questions and answer them aloud. Assistance should be given to the students if their answers are incorrect. After each page is completed, the students should evaluate their own listening skills and circle the number of smiles they feel they have earned for good listening. One smile is for good listening. Two smiles are for very good listening. Three smiles are for great listening.

Who is skating?
What are they skating on?
Where are they skating - inside or outside?
What kind of skates are they wearing?
When do you iceskate - in winter or summer?

Who is using a shovel?
What is he doing?
Why do you think he is shoveling?
Where is he shoveling?
Why is he wearing a scarf and hat?

Which children are drinking something hot?
What do you think they are drinking?
Where are they sitting - inside or outside?
What do you see falling outside the window?
When does it snow - in winter or summer?

Who is riding on a sled?
Who is pulling the sled?
What is being used to pull the sled?
What do you see on the ground?
When do you use a sled?

Great Ideas for Teaching!   AUDITORY PROCESSING OF "WH" WORDS

STUDENT WORKSHEET

Name: _____

Great Ideas for Teaching!   AUDITORY PROCESSING OF "WH" WORDS

61

INSTRUCTOR'S WORKSHEET

DIRECTIONS: Before beginning, each student should be given a copy of the student worksheet that corresponds to this instructor's worksheet. Start with any picture and its group of questions. Ask the entire group of questions under a picture before going on to another picture. The students are to look at their working copy while they listen to the questions and answer them aloud. Assistance should be given to the students if their answers are incorrect. After each page is completed, the students should evaluate their own listening skills and circle the number of smiles they feel they have earned for good listening. One smile is for good listening. Two smiles are for very good listening. Three smiles are for great listening.

Who is holding a cake?
What kind of cake is she holding?
Why are there candles on the cake?
What do you do when you blow out the candles?

Who is taking a walk?
Where are they walking?
Why is the mother holding the little boy's hand?
What kind of day is it - sunny or cloudy?

Who is baking something?
What is she baking?
What is she using to stir the batter?
Where will she put the batter when she is done stirring it?

Which people are having a picnic?
What are they sitting on?
Where are they keeping their food?
Who do you think made the picnic lunch?
What are they eating for lunch?

Great Ideas for Teaching!   AUDITORY PROCESSING OF "WH" WORDS